Lifestyle of an Alco

CW01083420

I would like to thank all the people who have entered my life, be that good bad or indifferent as without them there would be no book. I would also like to thank God that I have lived to tell the story.

To protect the identity of individuals, I have changed the names of people and places.

Email: **catherineerellison@gmail.com**

Enjoy

Lifestyle of an Alcoholic Woman

Contents

Would I Ever Escape?

I would like to think that this book would make an interesting, thought provoking, emotional roller coaster of a read for anyone. Nevertheless, in particular if you or a loved one is struggling with addiction, domestic abuse or mental health issues I don't doubt that you will find this book useful, informative, funny and at times shocking. I also expect this book not only to change lives, but also to save lives. I need to tell you that this story was taken from my best-selling autobiography *"Change or Die: Abuse to Addiction to Abundance."* Obviously with a few adjustments so that it can stand on its own and make sense. Some of the content is also in another book I wrote, so if you have already read *"Domestic Abuse: I Eventually Turned*, you will find some repetition. That said, let's get on with this story.

I was twenty years old, with my two year old son when I left my husband and moved from a small Northumberland town to Newcastle upon Tyne. Now I know that sounds young to already be married, separated and have a two year old and so it was! My mother had died when I was seventeen and my father had left the family home years before her death. A housing association provided me and my son David with a bedsit. This was a one roomed first floor apartment with very high ceilings, there was a shelved

Would I Ever Escape?

cupboard in the corner which acted as a pantry. A shared bathroom and toilet could be reached down several dark old wooden stairs which passed the doorways of other residents. I bought a bed-settee which acted as a bed for the two of us in the evening. A two ring old electric cooker with a sink stood in the corner of the room. I also had an old fashioned boiler for David's nappies and a small spin dryer to put the clothes in after they were washed in the kitchen sink by hand! A fourteen year old girl Susan lived with her grandmother in one of the upstairs apartments. Her mother was dead; it was never clear if she had been murdered or if it was suicide. Susan was a tall, well-made girl with shoulder length, thick, wavy brown hair, she was a bonny young girl who almost always wore a smile. She was a breath of fresh air and frequently knocked on my door to see if I needed a baby sitter. Given, she was a seasoned baby sitter for her large family, I usually allowed her to look after David while I went out. Shortly after meeting her I gradually got to know the rest of her very large family. One of her uncles called Jeff asked me out. I accepted and we agreed that he would call down for me on his way out that evening while his niece Susan babysat. He arrived hours later than agreed; I was getting quite wound up waiting on him. Little did I know then that this was

Would I Ever Escape?

going to be how my life would be for the next fourteen -
years.

Although my childhood was dire, the next fourteen years
with this man were worse. He was ten years older than me
and took advantage of my naivety. I even believed that in a
fight it was not fair to cheat; that is, I had to fight fair with
my hands. Needless to say I didn't have a chance, he was
almost 6ft and 14 stone. I weighed in at 5ft 1inch and 8
stone. The odds, very like my childhood, were once again
stacked against me.

Shortly after we met we were invited to a function at the
Mayfair dance hall in Newcastle. While at this event I lost
contact with him, and as I couldn't find him, I decided to
make my way home. When I returned to his mother's flat
he was waiting. He called me all the sluts and accused me
of meeting someone else and having sex with him. He
punched me in the face and chased me out of his mother's
house. I went to my own apartment downstairs. I locked the
door and swore to myself that I would never have anything
more to do with him, or any man who ever hit me.

It was about 10 am the next day when he came knocking at
my door. I refused to open it and said I wanted nothing
more to do with him. I heard a thud, then another. Gosh he

Would I Ever Escape?

was kicking the door in, I was terrified. He burst into my flat and beat me up quite badly. He said, "*If you go to the police they cannot give you twenty four-hour protection. I will find you and make such a mess of your face that no one will ever look at you again.*" This man was frightening. He said he was going for a pint and would be back, a bit like Arnold Schwarzenegger. I was in a terrible state and too frightened to contact the police. He was right, they could not give me 24 four hour protection. He came back in the early hours of the morning, that was hours later than expected, and just behaved as though he had a right to live in my apartment and for me to be providing for him.

What had I got into? This question never entered my mind. I did not know the meaning of reflection. Not only was the action not in my repertoire of behaviour, the word was not in my vocabulary. It was just a complete rebound from my childhood, the only skills I had were for survival, which consisted of going from one catastrophe to another. Although I was already quite a heavy drinker I started to drink heavier. If he was out I would mix Brown Ale and Old English cider to make snake-bites, drinking this concoction until my mind was dull or obliterated. This was one sure way to avoid feeling the punches and kicks he

Would I Ever Escape?

would throw when he eventually returned from his night out.

Many a time I would be unconscious before he got back, and if not I would try to pretend I was sleeping. I learned to sleep on my stomach to protect my face from the blows. Sometimes I tried to fight him back, but I was no challenge for him. After the first time this man hit me I did say to him, "If you ever harm a hair on my son's head I swear I will leave you for dead." All the years I was with him he never smacked or hit David. I think he knew that what I had said was no idle threat. Now I think you might wonder how I could find it in me to protect my son and not myself. My only explanation would be that, I think I would definitely have murdered for my son, where I believed I had to fight fairly in a fight. I suppose that was the mentality I was brought up with.

When I met Jeff I was still working at a hotel in the city. He would repeatedly accuse me of having sex with the men in the hotel. I was naive and spent most of my time trying to defend myself. I would be stupid enough to try to reassure him that was not the case, that was not something I would do. On reflection, I wish I had smashed him over the head with a cricket bat, even a rounders bat would have

Would I Ever Escape?

done! Never mind, hindsight is a fine thing, only thing was at that time in my life I didn't understand how men like him used these tactics to control their partners.

In my day there was not such a thing as a computer in homes, never mind the internet, so I was definitely on my own. Women were also shamed if they badmouthed their partner or even discussed their relationship with others. Relationships were considered sacred and even the police seldom interfered, as couples had to sort out their own affairs! The constant putdowns, accusations, violence and threats of more violence shattered my self-esteem, confidence and any smidgen of self believe I might have had, before meeting him. When we were out, I was terrified in case another man might look at me, as I knew only too well the consequences of that when we got back in the house.

Yes, hindsight is a fine thing, but like reflection it was not in my repertoire of behaviours. I felt trapped and violated in this relationship, with no escape. He acted as though I was his property to do with whatever he wanted. Although I'd always worked, my money was no longer mine. I had to work to give him money, as without his beer money life was completely unbearable. One day he beat me up so

Would I Ever Escape?

badly that I was unrecognisable; I looked more oriental than English. My eyes were black and blue and so swollen they just looked like small slits. Whenever he injured me he would not let me out of the house to get medical attention, yes he was very protective of his reputation!

During this time my son David attended a local nursery, fortunately in some strange way he was sheltered from most of the violence and aggression. Although it was impossible to protect him from all of the fights. On one occasion when he was staying at Jeff's sisters' he heard us coming in from the bar. The snow was lying thick on the ground, Jeff and I started to fight. He punched me in the face and knocked me over the neighbour's wall. David was only four years old; he ran at Jeff with his fists flying, crying, "I hate you, I hate you." David was a quiet, gentle soul and from ever I can remember people would say, "If the world was full of David's we would have a really good world." I know you are probably thinking that he should never have been subjected to these experiences in the first place, and I totally agree. My dreams for our ideal lifestyle had certainly been absolutely shattered.

During this period, if I was not at work. I would drink night and day the same as him. I would take David to nursery in

Would I Ever Escape?

the mornings, and would join him in some bar and just drink. Often on the way home from the bar he would call at the betting shop. He would ask me for all the money I had, and begin to gamble it away. Many times we were left without a penny, but I would always have put a few shillings away so that I could buy food. I had promised myself that my son would never go hungry and he never did. Jeff would always find a way to get his drink money for that night. I would realise days or weeks later that he had sold something from the house. Usually someone would come up and say, "Oh that thing that you sold us is great." I would be surprised, as I had sold them nothing. Jeff would tell someone that I was selling some of my belongings from the house to get the money for his drink. He was a compulsive liar, time and time again I would find things out through other people. I never failed to be confused as to why someone might lie repeatedly. What an unshakable, foolish, faith I had in human nature.

We eventually moved to Scotland beside some of his family. I thought things might improve. I had to be the eternal optimist! Do I need to tell you there was no change? We stayed with his auntie on his father side, she thought he could do no wrong. She would hear the fights going on between us and never interfere. He kept up his torrent of

Would I Ever Escape?

violent, physical and verbal attacks on me. He never stopped making accusation that I was having sex with anyone and everyone. On reflection many years later, it was obvious that he used this method of violent bullying, controlling behaviour to camouflage his insecure, cowardly personality. One day I was on a bus with him, I swept my long dark hair out of my eyes with my hand. He waited until we got home then accused me of waving to an ex-boyfriend. Would you be surprised if I said that was just another excuse to kick me all over? It was these experiences that made me really appreciate how lovely my mother was!

One night when we were fighting he punched me in the face and hurt my arm. The next day I went to the hospital thinking I had broken my arm, as it was really sore. The doctor asked me to move my arm in various directions which I did. He eventually said, "Your arm is not broken, but your jaw is." It is amazing how a more severe pain overrides a lesser pain. "No" I said, "It's me arm." thinking the doctor was stupid. Alas, he had hit me so hard in the mouth that my jaw was all broken. When asked how this had happened, I had to say, "I fell and hit my face on the edge of a pavement." Once again I knew only too well the consequences if I told the authorities what really happened.

Would I Ever Escape?

I was told in no uncertain terms that this injury was not caused by a fall on the pavement, and would more likely to have been caused by a very hard punch in the face. I was admitted to hospital, as the break needed an operation and I was unable to eat anything except strained food. I could only open my mouth a tiny bit, and if by accident I tried to open it too far the pain was excruciating, shooting right through me.

Another day when we were fighting he put all my clothes up the chimney and covered them in soot. I did just as well, I soaked his every possession in a bath of water with everything I could find in the bathroom. That included the bleach, vim, toothpaste, perfume, and anything else I could lay my hands on. Sometimes I could laugh when I looked back at the shenanigans. To be fair it was not all doom and gloom, although the good times were few and far between. Without a doubt he was the embodiment of misery, other than when he was holding the bar up. In this environment he was always the life and soul of the party. Everyone thought he was such a good man, a fun loving jack the lad. That is those who didn't live with him held this opinion. You will have guessed by now it is not the opinion I held of him.

Would I Ever Escape?

On numerous occasions I ended up with nowhere to live, and was not unfamiliar with the procedure for applying for homeless accommodation. Sometimes the violence was so bad I could not go home. One night after we had been out drinking, and he'd started to fight I had climbed into an old car in a scrap yard to get away from him. That was fine until I woke up the next morning with a German shepherd barking. I don't know yet how I got in there, but believe me I didn't dally on my way out or I would have ended up as breakfast for Fido. Another time I slept in the cemetery – well in the church doorway as I guessed that would probably be the safest place to be, as I did not imagine anyone would go there. This time I woke up to the sun shining. My luck was in!

I eventually moved in with a member of my family who had moved to Scotland. They loved having David staying and were very happy to babysit when I did go out. I had to continue in the relationship with him or he would have plagued my family. Men like that are unable to let go of the relationship and will go to extremes to keep "their" partners exactly where they want them. They thrive on the control and power they possess through their violent bullying behaviour. Did you know that in 2018, after women left their partners 80 were killed by their former male partner

Would I Ever Escape?

in England, Wales and Northern Ireland. Although I am going back many Yes, the terror of leaving the relationship was embedded in my brain, with the constant barrage of threats about what he would do to me when he found me. The other threat that plays, havoc with the mind is: "*I will make such a mess of your face, no one will ever look at you again*". This sort of threat is really scary, especially when living with a man who is already beating you up and pays no regard for the law.

Would you be surprised if I told you that eventually my health started to deteriorate? I went down to six stone in weight and began to go psychotic. I was having a complete breakdown, although I had no idea of what was going on. I had lost touch altogether with reality. I found myself standing in a job centre just looking at the jobs board unable to read any of the words. Everything in my brain just seemed completely muddled up. When I tried to speak the words would not come out my mouth. I was hallucinating and imagined this man doing me all sorts of harm; perhaps I wasn't imagining this! My brain had gone into a state of fear and shock, brought on by years of abuse. I did eventually get home and spent the night wondering around talking out loud without any idea of what I was

Would I Ever Escape?

saying or doing. Eventually they telephoned a doctor and sent for an ambulance.

They took me by force to a psychiatric hospital in Ayrshire. This was one of the biggest fears of my life; my nightmare was now happening. This hospital had all the echoes of my childhood when they locked my mother up. I had to escape. Not long after being admitted I was walking along a corridor on the second floor when I spotted a heavy table lamp. I picked it up and smashed it as hard as I could through the window. As the glass fell to the ground I followed it. Unfortunately I was unable to fly and hit the ground hard as I landed. The glass cut into the flesh on my foot, obviously producing a lot of blood. I tried to get up to continue my escape bid, but the pain in my ankle was excruciating, I was unable to stand. Still determined, I crawled around the grounds looking desperately for an escape route, leaving a trail of blood as I went. Drat my luck was out, a hospital groundsman found me, and I was taken back to a ward. I lay for days with my foot three times its normal size. I was unable to stand because of the pain and practically crawled everywhere. It was days later when my sister arrived. As she walked into the room she looked with horror, as I lay with my leg up on a bed unable to put on any socks or shoes. She asked if they had taken

Would I Ever Escape?

me to a general hospital for an x-ray. She was furious when I told her in my slow, slurred, and drugged up voice that no one had done anything. She demanded that they get me to a hospital immediatcly for an x-ray. After her intervention I was taken to a general hospital and my ankle, which was badly fractured, was put in plaster. I was escorted back to the psychiatric hospital with a pair of crutches, at least I could now get around, although much to my dismay not as fast as I would have liked.

I was held against my will in this hospital for months, I hated it, even on crutches my thoughts never wavered too far from my next escape. I learnt that years later a lot of cases of abuse were brought to the fore about this particular hospital, which I can assure you did not surprise me one little bit.

I was now left with no more contact from my family. Because the hospital was very difficult to get to, and most of my family lived in the North East of England I had no way of knowing what was going on. I was told nothing about my son or my family. I felt completely cut off from the world. I also had none of my own personal belongings whatsoever with me, nor did I have access to any money. Because of my frequent attempts to escape I was sectioned

Would I Ever Escape?

under the Mental Health Act. This meant they would not let me out of the hospital and could treat me against my will. They forced me to take medication which made my head feel as if it was in a cage. This certainly left me with a 'real' understanding of what people meant by chemical cosh. I discovered first hand that they did not need to hit me over the head with a truncheon in order to reduce me to a comatose state.

I was desperate to get out of this place and made numerous attempts to escape, but because the hospital was in a rural setting it made my attempts so much more difficult. I would find some way to get out of the hospital grounds; and when I thought it was safe I would start to hitchhike along the road. A car would eventually stop and I would jump in delighted with myself. "Yes I'm free." The car would turn around and take me straight back to the hospital; I think the staff patrolled the highways looking for escapees. That's when you know your luck is out.

Eventually they decided I was well enough to be allowed out of the hospital for the weekend. How charitable! They provided me with enough medication to last the weekend and I had to return on the Monday. They gave me a bus pass for the journey from and back to the hospital. I went to

Would I Ever Escape?

where my son was staying with family; they had been informed I was out for the weekend. During the weekend, I threw the medication down the sink, took my son for a walk and never went back. I hitchhiked over two hundred miles down through Glasgow and back to Northumberland. On my way through Glasgow I encountered a gang of Glaswegian teenagers. They asked why I was hitchhiking with a wee boy. Of course I didn't tell them I'd just escaped from the mental hospital. Can you imagine it? Nevertheless, the few shillings they had they tried to force me to take to help with my journey. Now although I wouldn't take their money, they certainly left their mark in my heart. To be fair, at that time in my life I did not have much of a heart! When I got back to the North East I stayed for a few days with an auntie, before going back to live with my husband. We lived in a farmhouse surrounded by the Cheviot Hills. A few months ago I went back to see this cottage and stood spellbound by the beautiful surroundings. Surroundings which all the time I lived there I could not see. I never once noticed this amazing scenery. That is just an indicator of where my head was at during this period.

We had a couple of neighbours who lived in the farm cottage next door; they were young and good fun. During this period I used to cook some great meals. My neighbours

Would I Ever Escape?

thought my cooking was fabulous - I would make the best ever soups, broth, dinners, home-made quiches and bacon and egg flans. Family and friends would come miles just to enjoy my food. I told no one what had happened to me in Scotland, not even my husband. I was so ashamed, and frightened of being caught that for the next twelve years I kept my ordeal a close secret. I also thought I would be on a missing person's file; which meant the police would be looking for me to return me to that God forsaken place. This seriously affected what I did, as the experience had really knocked my confidence and also left me doubting my sanity. I reasoned that as they were reluctant to allow me to live back in the community, there must be something mentally wrong with me! One thing I did do was pray earnestly every day and night that I would never go through anything like that again as long as I lived.

Nevertheless, although our life style was quite good everything was not working out in our relationship. As a result of our differences my reunion with my husband did not last very long; although we did not fall out we agreed to separate again. My time in the area did last long enough to establish myself, and get a two bedroomed house in a lovely village near Berwick. In my new house on the outskirts of the village pheasants used to walk passed the

Would I Ever Escape?

door in the morning. When I walked up the street everyone would almost sing, "Good morning". This was such a contrast to what I was used to. My immediate neighbours had bought their council house and the majority of residents were from middle class backgrounds. In fact, as the village was so small there was not even a bad area. Had I gone up in the world?

I felt good living in the village; it was a safe friendly and pleasant place. David was a shepherd in his first school play. On the day of the play all of the other children's mothers and fathers had arrived on time. I walked in after the play had started and tried to sneak into a back seat without being spotted or causing any fuss. David saw me as I entered the room and screeched with excitement. "There's me ma." Well if I could have crawled into a corner I would, as every head in the room turned to see who was so important that I got this special welcome. That day always brings a smile to my face. Nevertheless, you've probably guessed, I was soon to end our idyllic life style.

The Road to Ruin

It was now 1979; I was twenty-six years old and working as an extra on a Walt Disney film with David. Yes, I did say a Walt Disney film. Things were going really well; I had my youngest sister and a girl from Scotland staying with me. One day when I was at my auntie's house, I noticed some letters lying and recognised the handwriting, they were addressed to me. I felt bewildered, as I asked what she was doing with my letters. She said they were from Jeff. I picked the letters up and said I was angry that she had thought it was all right to open my mail. My auntie and sister said they had done it to protect me from him, as they hated seeing me with black eyes and bruising all over.

Me being a sucker, I read the letters which were written with what appeared to be great affection and sincerity. They were written in a way that someone naïve or just completely stupid like me would be taken in by the flattery and seduction. Yes, they were 'love letters' at their best. He said, how much he was still 'in love' with me, and if only he could have another chance everything would be so different. He would never again abuse or hit me. If only I knew how much remorse he felt. He promised that if we tried again there would never be any fighting; he had

The Road to Ruin

learned his lesson. He would even make up for all the bad things he had done. Well I can hear you thinking, surely, she is not stupid enough to believe this baloney.

Guess what, me being such a trusting soul with great faith in human nature, you know the sort of person who believes people change, (without years of therapy or divine intervention) we ended up back together. He was sweetness and light itself for the first few weeks. It was not long before he moved back in with me, and it would not take Einstein to work out that the fighting and rows soon started all over again. He would drink in the local pubs and have lock-ins until about two in the morning, or sometimes not bother coming home. I found I was working all hours in three jobs to keep us going in food, drink and gambling. The years were passing me by and I absolutely hated my life, going back to him was the biggest mistake I'd ever made. Once again I was trapped, battered, abused and constantly subjected to a stream of verbal abuse.

One day he was going on and on about money for drink and I said I did not have any. Because I refused to give him money he threw a heavy mug at my face. I moved and the mug smashed off the wall and into the back of my head. I thought I was going to die because of the amount of blood I

The Road to Ruin

was losing. The blood had saturated my white blouse and was running down my underwear. I had to get out and get the split in my head stitched. That time, I did eventually get out of the house, even though he was trying to stop me so that no one knew what a b...... he really was. I think he eventually realised that this deep gash could not go without medical attention. Whatever you do, don't think that he bothered to come with me to the hospital; that would have been expecting too much. It was enough for him to let me out of the house. I walked from where we lived to the local hospital with the blood pouring out my head. They had to shave my head and stitch it up.

The staff at the hospitals always asked how I had been injured. This was where I had to think up some excuse to cover his behaviour. I knew only too well the consequences if he found out I had told them what had really happened. That particular day I was really fed up, and knew he would have gone to the local pub while I was at the hospital. I deliberately walked into the pub on my way home, and sure enough there he was, the life and soul of the party. Well I burst his bubble that day, as I made such a scene exposing his brutality. I made it clear that the blood that saturated the blouse I was wearing was a result of him smashing a cup

The Road to Ruin

into my head. Believe me I was not top of the popularity list, but I was beyond caring.

I can hear you saying why on earth did you not get out of this relationship? Well I will tell you. I lost count of the times I tried; I moved house countless times, I would find somewhere else to live, and when he was out I would either pack up my belongings or just move with nothing. I would start building up a new life and be really pleased with myself, as things began to improve. My son and I would be living in a peaceful environment looking forward to a future. It would not be long before I would hear a knock on my door, when I went to answer it he would be standing. My heart would drop to my toes with disappointment, fear and resentment. I felt like Julie Roberts in the film 'Living with the Enemy'. All my dreams would be shattered once again. If I refused to let him in he would make threats, and if I shut the door on him he would just kick it in, or smash a window and come through that. I couldn't win.

In those days few people had telephones in the house, so it was not as though I could phone the police as he was kicking the door in. Once he knew where I lived I knew there was no escaping him. I think he believed that I was his property because we had been in a relationship. A bit

The Road to Ruin

like women are something you own, not individuals in their own right. I felt alone with no one in my corner and no one caring a dot whether I lived or died. Unfortunately, I knew he was not going to leave voluntarily, that would be too much to expect.

Over the years I lost count of the times I hitchhiked around the country. Jeff would go off with the money we had with the promise of returning, or worse still I would realise he had disappeared and so had the money. He would usually have the week's food money in his pocket which I knew he intended to spend on his drink. I was lucky that nothing too dangerous ever happened during these journeys; other than one day an elderly woman gave us a lift. She had no windscreen wipers and there was a massive blizzard. After she stopped the car a number of times in the middle of the road, because she could not see, and needed to get out to wipe the windscreen. I eventually said, "Thank you but I will take my chances waiting in the blizzard." I have been so lucky in many ways, as my son was a gem; he was and still is so easy going and laid back. I think it was his way of keeping some equilibrium in a crazy household. Although he was not interested in books or academia he had and still has a wisdom which seemed to pervade every part of his being. He does tell his friends some of the things

The Road to Ruin

I did bringing him up, but never in a bad resentful way; although I am sure if he did he would have every right to. Sometimes if his friends are in the house he will say, "Mam tell them about the time …" I think most of his friends had more normal mothers during their childhoods!

Nevertheless I continued to work in both paid employment as a carer for the elderly, and for myself. I was quite an entrepreneur and sold all sorts of things, I bought kippers and fresh fish from North Shields fish quay and sold them in the bars around the city. With the money I made I became more adventurous investing in a set of weighing scales. Now I could buy fruit and veg from the wholesalers. I would put about three pound of potatoes, a cabbage, turnip, carrots, apples, oranges, bananas and some salad in a bag and sell it for a £1 around the doors. At first I was restricted to delivering as many bags as I could carry as I had no transport. Never fear as help was on its way, some local kids knocked on my door with a railway trolley to help me to deliver the fruit and veg parcels. How good does it get? My business was now growing I could deliver even more parcels. This growth resulted in the progression to a bump start transit van. That is, I had to park it on a hill so that I could roll it into a start, or the alternative was the whole street had to come out to push it before it would

The Road to Ruin

bump start. Now the kids could deliver the railway trolley back to British Rail, and I could get on with a bit more serious business. What do they call it? Business development! Over the years I had umpteen cars and vans. Many, but not all were old bangers which needed a constant stream of parts which I would buy from the scrapyards. I became a dab hand at climbing over the top of car roofs in a pair of high heels, which I always wore! These were the days when you could buy an MOT for £40, and we could fix the exhaust pipe on the car with a beer can and two jubilee clips! Innovation and creativity in abundance.

My next venture was when the some lads came banging on my door really excited. "Catherine there's a shop for sale; it sells second hand goods, it will be a great business for you and Jeff." I went up to the shop and sorted out the finances. I think he was selling for a few hundred pounds which I was able to organise. It wasn't only MOTs which could be bought, in those days you could buy pay packets and pay slips. An authenticated worn look was achieved by scrunching them up as they were rubbed on to a dusty floor. This was the resourceful method used by the locals to organise loans. Fortunately I have always hated having debt, and was lucky enough to make sure I could work to

The Road to Ruin

pay for the things I wanted in life. I gave the guy the money he wanted, and started selling second hand furniture. I was now working night shift as a carer for the elderly, and running the shop through the day. I occasionally fell asleep when working alone in the shop. One day a man had looked in, and went to seek Jeff from the bar because I was lying with the door of the shop wide open fast asleep. The shop was in a very deprived rundown area of the city; and certainly not the sort of place to be lying sleeping. However, I was so exhausted trying to work night and day to provide a decent living for David my son and myself; as well as bringing in enough money for this tyrant of a man who beat me up if I did not have enough drink money for him. If he stayed in and watched the television he would sit and shout obscenities at the programmes. His cascade of verbal obscenities was so disturbing to listen to I felt sick at times. I think this was his Neanderthal understanding of what it was to be a man. My take on his behaviour today was more in line with a psychopathic, narcissistic, low life prat.

Often the young lads who weren't at school or working would ask to do jobs. If they saw me bringing a delivery in they would be there to give a hand. I used to give them money to buy food at the Greggs 'seconds' shop across the

The Road to Ruin

road. Jeff came and went as and when he wanted. He liked playing the business man, but was never there to do the work. As often as not I moved the furniture myself; this included every household item you could imagine: tables, armchairs, sofas, wardrobes, beds, drawers and mattresses. When I started this business I bought a transit van and progressed to a Luton. If I wasn't emptying houses, I was buying from Millar's auction rooms. I was also turning over enough money to keep us afloat and him off my back.

Sometimes after work I would go to the bar. One night a fight broke out. A young woman went to hit an older woman who I knew and liked, it was actually one of Jeff's family. I jumped over the bar table and grabbed her to stop her hitting this woman. Inevitably, we ended up in a fight which I won. I did not give it another thought. However the next night I was getting ready to go out when my friend came rushing in. "Where are you going?" she shrieked in a concerned voice. "I'm going out." I replied, surprised at the urgency in her voice. "You can't go out, there are about two hundred of them on the pub corner." She shrieked. "Well I'm not staying in, that's for sure." I told her. She told me to wait until she got her family to make some telephone calls. They telephoned a number of bars in the East and West End which included The Raby, Jacksons,

The Road to Ruin

The Bobby Shaftoe, The Cumberland Arms, Blue Man, Robin Adair, Dodds Arms, and the Chesterfield. I made my way to the pub where I was met by quite a reception. The bar was heaving with dozens of familiar faces. We waited on trouble starting, I sat with my back to the wall facing the door. This was in order to see anything that might erupt. Alas the night ended quietly, I must say I did not feel alone that night. Crazy as it may seem I think it was also this dynamic along with his family which kept me going.

A year after we got back together I realised I was pregnant. Yes, this left me in a dilemma, I really did not imagine spending the rest of my life with Jeff; yet on the other hand I was so pleased and looking forward to having another baby. I had always imagined myself with lots of children like my auntie, eleven would do! I bought in all the things I needed, as you can imagine there was nothing left from David's childhood. I felt quite excited during the pregnancy looking forward to a new baby. However, I was told by the consultant, that given the problems I had experienced at David's birth that there was a high chance of me dying during the delivery. He said, I would be better off having an abortion. I refused and said I would leave that decision in God's hands, as I did not believe I had the right to take my babies life.

The Road to Ruin

Although the small village where I lived was fifty-six miles from Newcastle, I was in Newcastle when my waters broke; I was rushed into the local hospital. Things started to go wrong, my blood pressure was soaring and once again the situation moved into dangerous territory. This time I remained conscious. I could feel my baby being born, although he came feet first instead of head first. After he was delivered they handed him to me to hold. What a precious little soul, he seemed to give me a little wink and his finger was sticking up as though he was telling me something. I had to smile. I felt absolutely delighted that everything had gone so well without any real complications. They took my baby away to attend to him, and Jeff's sister came to see me. She smiled as she said, "Catherine you look radiant." I felt radiant, I was so happy. I asked her if they were able to locate her brother Jeff. She said that they were trying, but had not been successful. No surprise!

It was not long before a nurse came to see me; she said we are putting you in another room. They moved me from the ward and put me in a room by myself. I did not think anything unusual and just waited for the return of my baby. Someone else came and told me that my baby was very ill. He had haemorrhaged during the birth because he had

The Road to Ruin

osteogeneses of the bones. In short, this meant his bones were very fragile, and during the delivery his head had been damaged. They said he would probably die. Well when someone tells you this about your baby it is hard to believe, especially as he looked perfectly normal and also healthy. Never mind, I still prayed to God to make him all right. The doctors told me I could sit with him as long as I wanted. I went along to the ward and sat by his incubator. He looked fine, I held him in my arms and chatted away to him, I really could not see a problem. They asked about his father, and as far as I know the police were sent to try and find him. That would be to the local bars! Some more of his family arrived and said they did not know where he was. That failed to surprise me, he was probably inebriated propping some bar up performing his lovely guy image to an audience of equally inebriated admirers.

The first day passed and my baby was still alive. I still did not think he would die and continued praying. On the ward one of the nurses asked me what I was going to call him. I said, "I'm not 100% sure, I have a couple of names in mind and haven't decided." I can remember thinking there was no rush he would be here for a long time. The stupid woman said something like, "Do you not realise that this baby is going to die and needs a name now." I was gob

The Road to Ruin

smacked at her lack of sensitivity and abruptness. I
muttered something and walked out. Later a priest came
and asked if I would like the baby to have a blessing and be
baptised in case he died. I said, "Yes." And told the priest
his name was Paul. Still not thinking that anything would
really happen to him. I knew this was a formality if babies
were not well. The priest gave him a blessing and baptised
him. That was fine, as I continued to gently hold him while
chatting away quietly as he slept. The next day I went to
get something to eat and left him for a short while. I had
not been away long when someone came to ask me to
return to the ward where Paul was. I went back, and was
taken into a side room where there was a doctor holding
Paul. He said, "Paul is going to die soon and I would like
you to hold him as he dies."

When you carry a baby full term and they look perfectly
healthy it is hard to really believe that they will die. I took
hold of him and nursed him close to my body. It was not
long before I noticed the skin down one side of his body
slowly turn navy blue; he looked terrible. I was still holding
him when the blood spurted out of his tiny mouth; I got a
terrible fright. I did not know that blood really spurted out
of people's mouths until that day. The doctor said, "That's
it, he's dead." I handed him over to the doctor without

The Road to Ruin

saying a word, and walked out of the room. I was frozen, raging inside with a bitter coldness.

The next thing I remember was his family arrived, they had eventually found him, too late as usual. He came into the room with his mother. I told them to f... off. It was not long before a priest came and said, "I bless you my child." I told him to f... off too, I said, "Don't bother me with your f...... God he has just killed my baby. Now f... off." I went to leave the hospital the nurse was running after me shouting, "You can't go out like that you have had stitches you need to rest. I told her to f... off too. I had no money on me, because Jeff had taken all we had that week for his drink money. I walked out of the hospital and hitch hiked the 56 miles back to the small village where I lived. I was one angry, bitter woman.

I organised Paul's funeral to make sure he had a good send off. He had a proper funeral, all my family and friends, and all his family and friends came to his funeral. Remember I had said when my mother died that I would never cry for anyone. Well I did not cry, neither did I speak to anyone. I was just numb and raging inside. Every time I looked at other mothers with their children I was jealous and angry. I resented them having their children when mine

The Road to Ruin

was dead. After this I hated God; how could he do this? He had certainly gone down in my estimation after taking my child's life. I had now even managed to develop a tempestuous relationship with God. I would not speak to him; this lasted for over a year before I was able to put my bitterness and resentment aside.

Although I had drunk very little during the pregnancy, I now started drinking heavily again. The experience was another one which I pushed to the back of my mind, and did not discuss with anyone. I was living in an environment where feelings were not up for discussion, the drink served its purpose of obliterating the pain. I remember Jeff once saying to me, "If you looked at me like you are looking at that bottle of Brown Ale I would know you loved me." He was well deluded if he thought he was any competition at all for a bottle of Brown Ale. It won hands down, and was certainly the more desirable object of my love, clearly doing a lot more for me than he ever did!

You might wonder why people didn't step in and try to stop me drinking or help in some way. I was so attached to the alcohol it would have been the equivalent of someone trying to interfere in a relationship with someone who I was completely in love with. I would not accept any form of

The Road to Ruin

"interference" by anyone. I would lash out, if anyone mentioned I was drinking too much. I would rather fall out with friends and family than allow them to mention to me the states I was getting into with the drink. I was terrified in case I could not get access to alcohol.

I hear so often that someone has tried to help a friend or family member who has a drink problem, and they struggle to understand why they are being rejected. The relationship between an alcoholic and their alcohol becomes the most important relationship in the world. It is not their children, brothers, sisters, mothers, fathers or friends; they really don't matter as much as having a drink. The alcohol dulls the pain whether that be physical, emotional or mental. You will be perceived as a threat or the arch enemy if you try to stop someone drinking before they are ready. Most alcoholics are also in denial of having any problem at all. So other than being there for someone and encouraging them to talk about what is behind their drinking, you are probably going to have to wait until they hit their own bottom where ever that may be.

It can be heart breaking for family and friends to stand back and watch a loved one drinking themselves to death, but this is so often what happens. Time and time again in

The Road to Ruin

my work I watched and heard story after story of the complete helplessness felt by friends and family as they stood by watching their loved one either dying or destroying their life. I know some people think, well they are making a choice to drink, believe me it is not so simple. The alcohol is often used as a form of self-medication to cushion or stop feeling feelings. There is often a lot of buried pain being masked by the drink.

The other issue here is when people think it is fine just to have one drink. What they fail to understand is that once an alcoholic starts drinking, the alcohol then affects their brain lowering their inhibitions and ability to control their drinking. ~~thus making them want more alcohol.~~ I used to swear away everyone's life and make promises galore that I wouldn't ~~would not~~ get drunk. I meant every word I said, before I had a drink, as soon as I started drinking, I couldn't stop! This is because alcohol changes brain chemistry, which in turn impacts thinking. moods, behaviours and memory. There was a threshold, a bit like the point of no return, and once passed it I had to keep going. ~~Ask any alcoholic how many times they tried to stop drinking and they will tell you thousands. Because even they believe they can control their drinking and keep attempting to prove this without success. Nevertheless, there will always~~

The Road to Ruin

~~be an excuse as to why they failed, but they will assure you they will definitely succeed next time. And on it goes.~~ Friends and family often give up trying to help, as they feel they are fighting a losing battle. They often are, as each person has to reach their own bottom before they will accept, they have a problem and accept help. It is absolutely futile to try to talk to an alcoholic when they are drunk. Any communication has to happen when they are sober and if you are lucky compos mentis, because if they have been drinking, the probability is they will either back you off, or have no memory of the conversation the day after.

Insight over, let's get back to my story. ~~I remember working with a client who said he wanted me to stop him from drinking. I asked him how many times he had tried himself to stop. He sat and thought about the question, then said, "Thousands".~~

Over the years I lost count of the people who came to live with us. One young boy stayed for about a year while he was on a curfew from the courts. He was a lovely lad, and no bother at all. My sister and her boyfriend also stayed with us for about a year when they were teenagers, but me being quite a prude I would not allow them to sleep

The Road to Ruin

together. We took in a homeless man who Jeff brought back from the bar, He stayed for a couple of weeks, he had been a professor and his wife had died. He just left everything to his daughter who worked in India with Mother Teresa and hit the road. Jeff's niece, Susan her husband and three children often stayed with us; I thought the world of this family. Then my brother turned up, who I asked to leave when he threatened my sister with a boiling hot kettle of water.

When people were staying there was probably less violence from Jeff, but it did not stop altogether. He was a master of manipulation and deceit. He encouraged people to stay so that he could use this as an excuse to get money to go out drinking.

I often wished I was dead. That was because he continued to plague my life. I would stand looking out of the multi-story flat windows where his mother lived and think about jumping out. I hated my life with this man, he rubbished all my dreams. If I had a good idea, he would ridicule it and tell me not to talk so stupid. The only thing that made my life bearable was my work, and his family who I got along with and liked. I obviously had my own family who I loved very much, but they were not having such an impact on me.

The Road to Ruin

The only person I had a problem with was him, as he was the only person I was living with.

I eventually went to a solicitor and told him I wanted Jeff to leave the house because of his violence towards me. This was in September 1982. The solicitor sent a letter to him at my address and a copy of the letter to the local police. The letter, which I still have, read:

We have been instructed by Catherine… who has informed us that as a result of your violence to her she is unwilling and unable to put up with your presence in the house. We therefore request that you leave the house immediately and take with you your personal belongings. If this request should cause you to offer any more violence to Catherine, then immediate application will be made to the court for an injunction and you will be reported to the police. If you are determined to cause trouble for her then she is determined to make sure through lawful means that you are prevented from doing this. A copy of this letter has also been sent to the police asking them to ensure that you leave the property without any further harm to our client.

The Road to Ruin

The letter arrived and he would not read it. That was another attempt at getting rid of him which failed. Months later, one night as I was getting ready to go out with him, the police arrived at the door with a copy of the letter. I told them he had refused to read the letter, so they gave him the copy and asked him to read it. He said, I was completely stupid and was getting ready to go out with him. He told the police I did not want him to leave, as we got along well. He also added what he had said to me for years. How on earth did they think they could enforce the law and keep him from returning to my house and doing what he wanted without providing 24 hour protection which they were not going to do.

Again I was beginning to feel frightened. He said to me in his threatening voice, "Tell the police you don't want me to leave." I conjured up as much courage as I could and said, "I do want you to leave." In an angry voice he said, "But you are getting ready to go out with me." I said, "I would rather stay in and would be pleased if you never come back to my house." It was as though he did not understand a word I said, "You don't mean that" he replied in a surprised yet sarcastic voice. For some reason, this man actually thought I wanted him around. The reality was I hated him. He was the most miserable, aggressive, insufferable person

The Road to Ruin

I'd ever known. Far from being a bundle of fun, he was a liar, a cheat, a womaniser, drinker and a gambler whose misconception with reality was ruining my life. He had nothing going for him; yet he was struggling to comprehend that I might not wish to see him, that in fact I was seeing him only under sufferance.

He eventually left while the police were there, but returned that night, put my window out when I refused to open the door, and came back in. He tried to get into the bedroom but I now had a plan, which short of him smashing the door down he would not be able to get in. I pulled the bed across the room and put a piece of wood between the bed and the door. This jammed it solid, as the wedge went from the door to the wall. I was finally safe from him, until I came out of the bedroom.

Because of the constant bullying and putdowns I felt really stunted in this relationship. You know when you feel under employed? Well I certainly felt that. I knew I had potential yet was unable to get into a well-paid profession for a couple of reasons. I still had some fear of that psychiatric hospital finding me and taking me back! I also had no qualification. Me being the eternal optimist, I decided to do some "O" levels at the local college to see if I

The Road to Ruin

could change the course of my life. By God I certainly was a woman with ambition! Jeff as usual rose to the challenge like a true champ with his bombardment of obsessively jealous, abusive comments. He could not bear the thought of me bettering myself. "Oh who do you think you are?" "Are you trying to be clever? sneer, sneer. "You are too thick to pass any exams." His put downs were relentless. Never mind, I ignored them and continued with my course, as well as working in a well know very rough bar in the city. During this period, we had many a violent fight.

One day, I was in the shopping centre with my carrier bag full of books for college, and a black bin bag full of his clothes and belongings. He had been out drinking all night, and had not returned home the next day. I walked into the local bar and threw his clothes right across the bar top, smashing everything on the bar. I got into a verbal fight with the manager who was about six foot three, and built like a rugby player. He threatened to hit me if I didn't shut up and get out. I retorted with a loud. "Yea that is all you're good for, hitting women." That was my five-feet one inch and 8 stone talking.

You will have noticed by now that when I felt wronged, I really had trouble keeping my mouth shut. Even as a child I

The Road to Ruin

would rather take a beating than keep the peace, if I felt things weren't fair. Apparently, this is the trait of Sagittarians, they are known for their sense of fairness. Without a doubt I certainly met this criterion. I told the bar manger to keep Jeff there, as he had better not come back to me. Jeff told me to get out and stop showing him up. I started to shout at him that all he was, was a woman beater and not worth a w--k. He ran at me, and by this time we were outside the bar. I kept dodging him, he liked to look the nice guy in front of everyone, but he was failing drastically that day. I would not shut my mouth. All the books, pens everything in the carrier bag (that was my briefcase) were thrown all over the shopping centre, as it ripped apart under the strain of been smashed into walls and pillars, as I ducked and dodged his attempts to get hold of me. He decided the only answer was to go back in the bar and ignore me. I walked in behind him and ordered three bottles of brown ale which I started to drink with a vengeance. That afternoon the bar clientele were coming up to me saying, "A've fund this in the shoppin centre hen is it yours?" "Yes" I would say as I added another item to my collection of lost goods.

Another night he came home and began hitting me. He went on and on and on with his ridiculous accusations.

The Road to Ruin

Eventually he fell asleep on the settee. It was a rare occasion when I was stone cold sober, but on this particular night I was. After he fell asleep, I looked for the hammer to bash his brains in. Unfortunately, I was unable to find it, nevertheless I found the next best thing. The pressure cooker lid. You know the sort I am talking about. The big heavy metal lids with the pressure bit sticking out of the centre. I looked at his face as he lay there snoring and thought about all the years, I believed I had to fight fair. I had spent years of my life trying to win against someone who was twice my weight and height in a fair fight. I decided there and then that he had cheated me for years. He had a massive advantage, there was nothing fair about the fighting we had been doing. Well here goes, I lifted the lid as high as possible above his head and brought it down as hard as I could. Smack! It landed, it was the strangest feeling, as each time it landed, it suddenly stopped. I don't know why that would surprise me! I kept hitting him over the head with it. I can remember each downward blow as if it was yesterday. I then took it across his knees and ran out of the house. This time I had opened the door ready for my escape. I hid behind a wall on the estate and watched the house. About half an hour later he staggered out the house and walked towards his sister's house. I went back in and

The Road to Ruin

locked the door. I did not see him for days. I met his sister and niece a few days later, and she angrily said, "You could have killed our Jeff hitting him like that." Now although most of his family had been in court for malicious wounding and could be violent people, I responded with. "You didn't interfere all the years he battered me, don't interfere now." She walked away and there was nothing more said.

He returned after a few days and said he had never felt as much pain in all his life. I was so pleased, I told him if he ever hit me again, I would do the same again because he had to sleep. I waited for him hitting me again. It never happened he had received the message loud and clear.

Now I know that sounds all well and good, but the reality was that it took years before I had the confidence to believe the fighting wouldn't start again. I don't think the fear ever really left me, as I always thought, will he start tonight when he comes home. This is something I fully understood when working as a psychotherapist. People do not just feel frightened the day they get beaten, they live in the constant fear of being beaten, as they never know when the next stream of blows is going to come. Will it be tonight or tomorrow? The unknown is often more frightening and

The Road to Ruin

anxiety provoking than the known. I do like the quote, "Most anxiety is caused by a projection into the future." This is so true, as most of the time we fear what might happen before anything happens.

You might be wondering how I was able to go from one catastrophe to the next. Well, I managed this really easily, it was all I seemed to know. When I studied psychology, I gained a better understood of how the early years are repeated time and time again, until there is an opportunity to work through the old traumas held in the psyche. So far, I had not had any time or opportunities to work through anything. I was too busy trying to survive the chaotic life I was unable to escape.

Jeff's niece Susan, the one who used to babysit, now had three boys who I loved to bits; they brought so much joy into my life. They learned quickly the ways of life for the environment they lived in. I had just started a new job and bought a new car to go with the job. Now given it was a sales job I was carrying a briefcase; a real briefcase this time and not a carrier bag! In the area where Susan lived anyone's car who was unknown would be highly likely to be broken into, especially if you were dumb enough to leave a briefcase where it could be spotted.

The Road to Ruin

Most professional people actually refused to work in the area, because of the level of car break-ins and violence. Guess what, when I went back to the car, surprise the car window had been broken, and my briefcase was missing. My niece's little boy, who was about three at the time said, "Auntie Catherine I will find out who smashed your car window and belt them." I felt touched by his loyalty and bravery. He was obviously oblivious to his limitations in size and strength, but certainly did not allow this to handicap his imagination.

Given my 'privileged position' as an insider, the children on the street told me who had broken into the car. I went around to their house on the next estate, and in my best 'gangsterish' voice said, "I will give you five f...... minutes to give me my briefcase back, and pay for the broken windscreen. If you don't I will demolish your f...... house." Within a few minutes a woman came to the door looking quite worried. In a rather timid voice she said, "It was our Ricky who broke in, he didn't know it was your car. He thought it belonged to one of the social workers." She followed through with, "He will be back soon and I will make sure he returns it and gives you the money for the window." At this point this big useless looking man came around the corner shouting obscenities at me. I was

The Road to Ruin

well dressed in a scarlet red Jacket and skirt looking ever so professional! I told him in no uncertain unprofessional terms, he had better move his arse back into the house and get my briefcase or I would wipe him of the face of the earth. He went back in and brought the briefcase out. He had sawn through it. It was not even locked, that was about the size of the mentality of the low life criminals in that area. Needless to say, they quickly paid me for the damage to both the briefcase and the car window.

Just in case you hadn't worked it out the whole scene I was associated with, was one of petty crime, alcohol, gambling, parties and violence. The lads also always found ways to make money. Empty houses were stripped of their copper wire and other saleable goods such as, gas and electric fires, cookers, boilers etc. Scrap metal was found along the river beds where Vickers used to dump material from the factories. The old sleepers from the disused railway lines brought in a nights beer money, and collecting metal from the roadside or anywhere else always filled a few pints. They even paid the watchman to "watch" while they took the lead tiles off the roof. Shepard's scrap yard did a roaring trade.

The Road to Ruin

When I first went to live in the city the teenagers used to steal from people's yards and houses; they would also steal clothes from washing lines. I drummed it into them that this was wrong, it was never alright to steal from anyone. I strongly imposed my moral values on many of the younger generation, and believe it or not they listened. Many of the teenagers stopped stealing from people as they started to understand that the people they were stealing from were like themselves; they were struggling to feed and clothes their own families and children. They also began to understand that it was never alright to steal from anyone no-matter how rich or poor they might be. I was always pleased with myself if I influenced anyone in a good way as my own behaviour certainly left a lot to be desired at this stage in my life, but I did have principles.

One day as I was driving down a quiet road in the country. There stood the most beautiful stone-built house in its own grounds. A 'to let' sign on the huge wrought iron gate caught my attention. The first opportunity available I enquired about the property and was able to put a deposit down which secured it. I waited quietly and patiently until I knew Jeff would not be around to organise a furniture van. I collected David and made a quick escape. This was a really grand house; a farmer had built it for his family and

The Road to Ruin

moved out. The outside walls were made of new Cotswold stone, there was a huge living room with an open coal or log fire, and a beautiful oak beam mantel piece. There was also a very large country kitchen, separate dining room and four bedrooms. The bathroom was bigger than most living rooms I had lived in to date with a massive corner bath. The garden surrounded the whole house, and there was not another house within quarter of a mile.

I moved out of my house in an appalling area of the city into this delightful large house, two minutes' walk from the beautiful Northumberland coast line. I had done it! Once again, I was going to live happily ever after. Well, that is really not too realistic. Yes, you guessed, it was not long before he had tracked me down and was knocking on my door. That once more was the end of my 'happily ever after'.

We were now on the home brew; I would wake up in the morning and look at the empty beer glass with scum up the sides. I was smoking 50 cigarettes a day and through the night. My fingers were all burned, as well as everything else around me. Through the day I was working in a rest home in Whitley Bay. In the mornings' I would walk down the drive to open the big wrought iron gates, vomiting

The Road to Ruin

every step I took. Sometimes I would collapse after I stood up, the colour would drain from my face, I would turn white and slide down the wall. If I had been doing this for effect believe me it wasn't working, no one ever took any notice. One morning I went passed my turn off on the roundabout and being such a bright spark, instead of going right around the roundabout I reversed back around the roundabout.

His niece, her partner and three children came to stay with us. They loved it in this massive house with all the outdoor space you could dream of having. I loved having them, they brought a real joy to my life. If I walked in and one of the kids was crying that they had hurt their leg, I would throw them on the table and shout for the knife followed by, "Don't worry if I cut it off the pain will disappear with your leg. They would scream, "It's better auntie Catherine its better." We'd giggle and laugh. Certainly not fitting behaviour for an eminent psychotherapist, but we did have fun. His niece would say, "You know this house is calm until you walk through the door and within minutes it is like a tornado hit it." In my life time I don't know how many times that was said to me; it seemed to be a natural talent I possessed. Again, that house was always full, people came and went. We did make amazing home brew

The Road to Ruin

and on many a weekend there were up to fourteen cars on the driveway, while we partied and drank the night away. After a couple of years of country life, I decided to move closer to the city again; this was so that I did not have so far to travel to work. This time I 'bought' a flat in a sleepy little village not too far from the city. I got a full mortgage as I had no deposit.

The sleepy village woke up, as we partied and drank to all hours in the morning. People would come from all over for the parties, and stay up drinking half the night away. I was getting worse and worse with the drink, my head was constantly in turmoil; my memory was going, and I really did think I had brain damage, either that or early dementia. I was holding down a dead-end job with no prospects. The truth is I was completely falling apart at the seams.

Coming Around from an Alcohol Induced Psychosis

I was thirty-four years old when I was coming around from a three-day coma in a dull drab room. At first, I was unsure if I was alive, as my brain struggled to connect with itself. Yes, I am alive, I can feel my physical body as I move my arms. I opened my eyes slowly, I was in a room with tall bare murky yellow walls, surrounded by an old-fashioned cornice. I was lying on a high metal bed with white sheets, unsure if it was a jail or a hospital. I was aware of feelings I had never felt before running through my body. The only words I can use to describe them are sensual, I could actually feel my body as though it belonged to me. At the same time, I felt shocked and confused as feeling feelings in my body was an extremely alien state. Now don't get me wrong, if someone punched me, which often happened I would certainly feel that, but I mean deeper emotions.

I remember as a seven-year-old child promising myself I would never cry again and I had kept that promise to myself all of my life to this very day. The world just seemed a hard place to be and no one was ever interested in my tears. In fact, the people in my life who were supposed to be the ones who provided love and support were actually the people who just seemed to inflict pain. So, I'd done the

Coming Around from an
Alcohol Induced Psychosis

best I could from a young age to protect myself from the barrage of abuse constantly thrown at me, that way life was much more bearable. Now coming around and feeling feelings seemed not only strange, but somewhat scary as well as exciting.

I also felt as though I had a soul; I know that might sound like a strange thing to say but it is what I felt. Before this experience I did not know people had souls. Now although I was fascinated by the sense that I actually had feelings in my body and a new soul, my thoughts quickly turned to where I was. I really needed to work out how I had got there, wherever there was! I was not sure what had been happening to me, although intrinsically I knew it wasn't good, as I strained my brain to think. Slowly the memories of the days leading to ending up here started to return. I must add that I did not know at this time that I had been unconscious for three days; so, my memory took me back to what had been happening prior to this unconscious state.

I remember my evening drinking episodes (such an understatement) were really taking their toll on my physical and mental health. I had been drinking to obliteration every night of the week for over a year. Prior to that I had been drinking alcohol most nights for the past seventeen years

Coming Around from an
Alcohol Induced Psychosis

with the occasional break. Whenever I drank, I got drunk; I can't remember ever being able to go out and have only a couple of drinks and return home sober. When I say I got drunk, I mean I would usually drink until I was obliterated.

You know what it's like when your friends want to tell you about all your misdemeanours during your previous evenings drinking spree? Well believe me, their efforts to deter me from another drunken episode were definitely going to land on deaf ears. I absolutely could not bear to hear what I had done while drunk. I just got into the habit of singing at the top of my voice so that I couldn't hear a word they were saying; I just didn't want to know.

I was living a life I really didn't want, with a man who I really didn't want. I felt trapped in a violent, abusive relationship with no escape. If I wasn't drinking at home we'd usually be accepted as the select few for a lock in. This is the term used for the largely illegal state, when the pub doors get locked after hours and a select group of friends can sit around and drink to the early hours of the morning. The next day, someone would come up and tell me things like, "You were sitting on the bar stool and suddenly fell backwards to the floor completely unconscious. Or, "He hit you and you reeled over."

Coming Around from an Alcohol Induced Psychosis

It was a very rare occasion when I could remember going home and if I was unlucky enough to be relatively sober, I would be guaranteed to make sure I had access to a lot more alcohol at home. It was agony to go home not completely drunk and as the beatings were so unpredictable the alcohol cushioned the blows. Yes, I certainly used alcohol for self-medication it was a brilliant anaesthetic.

Now I know this is going to sound really peculiar but it is just how it was. It was not until I had tried to stop drinking, that I started to go psychotic. I was fine while I was drinking, but as the alcohol was leaving my system I was going downhill rapidly. If you can imagine what it is to have alcohol in your system around the clock, then suddenly it is taken away, well say no more. I do need to clarify something here. I did not drink around the clock. I think there is a misconception about drinking and alcoholism. I believe most people think in order to be classed as an alcoholic you have to wake up and have a drink and be constantly drinking throughout the day and night. That is not the criteria for a diagnosis for alcohol addiction. The amount drank and durations of drinking can vary for each individual, some people binge drink, that is they drink huge amounts in one go which can last for hours,

Coming Around from an
Alcohol Induced Psychosis

days, weeks or months. Other people stay topped up around the clock and may not appear drunk, although if the alcohol is stopped, they will experience withdrawal symptoms. If there are concerns it is always best to seek advice from a knowledgeable well-informed professional. AA also does a lot of great work, and given they have been down that road themselves they certainly have the experience. AA is also very supportive of people who go for help; what puts a lot of people off is the connection with a "Higher Power". I would never rule it out as I am so aware of all the good work they do.

My memories leading up to coming around in this place were beginning to return and they were clearly not going to be memories which I would be sitting around bragging about. Gosh this was getting scary, best leave it until I see where I am. I decided to get out of the bed and try the door to see if that would give me any clues as to where I was. I opened the door slowly and could see I was on a hospital ward of some kind. There was a nurse just outside the door, "Oh," she said, "You have come around." I asked her where I was. She told me, "You are in St. Joseph's Hospital." I felt a streak of doom and terror run right through my body. I was in the psychiatric hospital – the

Coming Around from an
Alcohol Induced Psychosis

asylum - where they used to put my mother. It was the most horrific place in the world as far as I was concerned; I would probably have been less worried if she had said I was in prison. At least in prison you would know when you expected to be released, but in these places, they could keep you there indefinitely. My brain whirled, what had I done? How had I arrived there? What had been happening? How long had I been there?

I took a brief flash through my childhood memories, to those horrifying times I had visiting this place in the early 60s. From the age of seven I would negotiate the eerie hospital corridors to take my mother her family allowance. The corridors were scattered with zombie like patients making unrecognisable noises, mostly walking with their shoulders stooped and their heads facing the floor with eyes that either stared into the ethos or jumped around without focus. I hated this place and had never in my worst nightmare imagined I would find myself here.

My mind now had no choice but to brave the journey back to what I was doing before coming around. I can remember many strange experiences, which I later found to be what they call detoxing and going through the Delirium Tremors, better known as the DTs or cold turkey. Just to let you

Coming Around from an
Alcohol Induced Psychosis

know, the DTs are a psychotic condition caused by the sudden stopping of the intake of alcohol or other drugs. When chronic alcoholics are going through withdrawals the typical symptoms they will experience are: tremors, hallucinations, anxiety and disorientation. This is the most severe form of alcohol withdrawal and needs to be medically supervised because there is a risk of death.

Well, I had no medical supervision and had been swirling through the above symptoms with no connection at all to reality. I can tell you I'd rather fall off the edge of a cliff than go through that experience again. I can certainly understand how alcoholics die during this experience. My memory took me to the "Shop Front" on Westgate Road in Newcastle; this was a meeting place for alcoholics who were supposed to be no longer drinking. A friend took me there, as I was so far gone at this stage I was now incapable of functioning as a rational human being.

Lydia the woman who ran the programme for alcoholics was surprised, "Women don't normally come here." she said in her dulcet tones. No, she didn't turn me away, as I just stood there looking glazed, and to be fair, I didn't really care whether or not women went there, I just needed help badly. My only interest was in stopping the mental

Coming Around from an
Alcohol Induced Psychosis

torment and horrendous feelings that had taken over my brain and body. I felt so bad, death would certainly have been the better option.

Lydia was a social worker, she was a very attractive tall woman, with large brown eyes and beautiful thick long dark hair. There was no doubt in my head she would have passed for a model had she chosen that for a career, over working with down and outs in the back streets of Newcastle. I liked her, and hung on to the hope that she would help me. It didn't matter that the place was stinking with the smell of men's stale alcoholic urine.

She said I would have to come daily to the unit before she could get me a place in the local detox unit. She explained, this was so that I could be given a supervised detox, as it would be too dangerous to detox me at home, given the amount of alcohol I had been consuming. She worked with me for about a week before she could get me a bed in Parkwood House in Newcastle. The Friday prior to my Monday morning admission to the detox unit, she told me to try to relax, and have a quiet time until she came to collect me on the Monday morning.

Coming Around from an Alcohol Induced Psychosis

A quiet weekend was not on the radar, in fact I probably had not had a quiet weekend since leaving the womb. This weekend was no exception, there was a constant stream of trouble brought to my door. Some of my friends had been in a big bar fight and put the barmaid in hospital. It was touch and go if she would live or die. They sent someone to my door in the early hours of the morning, they wanted me to go up to the police station to bail them out. The police would not allow them out until they had word from the hospital that the woman would live, because if she died, they would be charged with murder. Fortunately, she did live and they were released the following day.

By the time I met Lydia on the Monday morning I felt as if I was not going to last the day. She took me to the detox unit and introduced me to the staff, then left saying she would keep in touch to see how I was doing. When I was taken to the ward where the patients spent their time, I was surprised to find a number of people whom I already knew, from the bars in the city. This improved my ego and made me feel at home! I quickly made friends during my stay, mostly with people who were in the detox unit with drug addiction problems.

Coming Around from an Alcohol Induced Psychosis

I don't suppose you would be surprised to learn that I did not really know what I was doing during that time. I had lots of tablets on me that had been given to me with good intentions by a woman trying to help me; I don't know who was the most deluded, her or me. I was taking the tablets to try to make me feel all right, as I think this was probably the worst I'd ever felt in my whole life. That is saying quite a lot since I'd certainly had far from a simple paper round up to that date. I felt as if I was struggling to survive. The experience was suffocating, like going completely under the ground, or like drowning. I felt as though it was taking every inch of the strength I had to try to stay alive. I remember my kidneys seemed to be excreting brown slush, I thought my insides were going to fall out. Every bit of my body and mind felt damaged. I had known for a while that the drink was killing me. My liver was swelling up every night with the alcohol so badly that I had to loosen my clothing. My memory was starting to go, and I thought I had brain damage, it was as though I would talk and fill in the gaps without any real thought to accuracy. In other words, I had reached a stage where my brain and the words coming out of my mouth did not feel connected.

Coming Around from an
Alcohol Induced Psychosis

While in the detox unit I remember experiencing a feeling during the whole night in which my psyche seemed to be going down some sort of spiral. It was like some sort of unravelling of my memories but at high speed. I felt as if some sort of healing was trying to take place, but the healing was worse than the problem. I was also completely disorientated and hallucinating. However, the terrible things I was seeing and hearing seemed real, yet they were as far from reality as the earth turning upside down overnight.

Trying to put a time scale to my memories was putting a real strain on my brain, which would not have been difficult at that time, nevertheless I was getting there. I worked out that I had been on the detox unit for about a week, when in my wisdom I decided to stop taking all medication they were giving me, to prevent serious withdrawal symptoms. Little did I understand the serious consequences of this action. My body now started to react to this alien state, it had seldom been alcohol free for many years and was now unable to cope without alcohol. I remember beginning to go psychotic after stopping the medication too early. In my psychotic state I discharged myself from the unit, but did not know what I was doing or

Coming Around from an Alcohol Induced Psychosis

where I was going. It was now obvious that the stopping of the alcohol and the medication had triggered the DTs.

Oh, my thoughts have just been interrupted by a young woman who is dressed differently from the nurses. Although at that time I hardly had the word psychologist in my vocabulary, I assumed she may have been a psychologist or someone connected to the psychological profession. After I came around the nurse had sent for her to do an assessment on me. She walked into the ward and bombarded me with questions.

She wanted to know what year it was, and who the Prime Minister was. I thought - she thinks she is in the evening history lesson and I'm the lecturer. Nevertheless, I was not going to say this to her, as one experience of these people misusing their power was enough in this life time. And, although I talk with some bravado believe me, I was so vulnerable and scared in case I had a repeat of the previous hospital which had taken me months to escape from.

Nevertheless, when she got to the part where she asked me to say the seven times table backwards from a hundred. I laughed, or rather sneered and said, "You have to be kidding. I can hardly tell you my name, let alone say the

Coming Around from an Alcohol Induced Psychosis

seven times table backwards from a hundred." This rather brash confrontation did not stop me from feeling somewhat inadequate, as if I could not do what I was supposed to be able to do. I now think it would have been more practical if someone had examined her head instead of mine. Only an idiot would ask someone just gaining consciousness to do such a feat. It would be likened to asking someone with a broken leg to run a mile.

Good, this ill-informed woman left, hopefully to study history and never to return. I was now free to go back to my thoughts and continue to recollect my memories. I remembered going home; David my son was now sixteen and must have gone through a terrible time with me during that period. Believe it or not he had always known me to be strong and in control. Maybe I'm still deluded! Well, the point is that 11 years earlier, after I was locked up in the hospital in Scotland, I swore I would not drink through the day. The reasoning being that if I was sober through the day, I would be able to take care of him and social services would not be able to take him from me. This was my ultimate wisdom, never thinking that if I drank so much in the evening, I was probably drunk most of the following

Coming Around from an
Alcohol Induced Psychosis

day, thus keeping my level of alcohol topped up around the clock.

Trying to resist drinking was a painstaking experience as many of those who have ever been on a diet or addicted to anything would know. I would start to watch the clock in the early evening and tell myself, 'I will not have a drink tonight.' It was like having two heads, one egging me on to drink, and the other trying to get me to stop; 'Well, I will just have a little drink.' 'No, it is starting to really damage you.' 'One more won't hurt' 'Well you never stop at one.' 'Well I will, I swear to God I will not get drunk.' 'You know your brain is starting to go and so is your liver.' 'You must stop drinking it is killing you.' 'Well it might be better if I were dead.' This internal dialogue would go on and on tossing from I will to I won't, until I would make that last minute dash to the shop and get enough alcohol to knock out a horse for the night. That is, my normal concoction would be a couple of two litre bottles of Old English cider mixed with an equal amount of Brown Ale. Many pubs will not serve snakebites as they have the power to make people drunk a lot quicker and more potently than other brews, hence known colloquially as lunatic soup.

Coming Around from an Alcohol Induced Psychosis

I am sure many of you reading this will know only too well the fight that goes on in your head when you are trying to stop any form of addiction. Only hope you had more success than me in your fight against temptation, because I certainly wasn't winning mine.

Nevertheless, I had gone back home to David, who I have no doubt was pretty scared and confused as he watched my completely insane behaviour. Fortunately, even though he was sixteen, that age when young people often go off the rails, he had his feet firmly on the ground. He needed them there, as mine were certainly not on the ground. One of us had to keep some sanity, and I can assure you I didn't have any. I thought the dog was the devil, and was planning vicious attacks against me. I'm not sure what the dog thought about me, as I chased him around the streets shouting and locked him out of the house! Perhaps he thought I was the devil planning vicious attacks against him. It would have been more accurate. I was talking to the pictures on the wall; that was because they were talking to me! Every programme on the television, even the news bulletins were addressed directly to me. Now would that be paranoia or narcissism? Everything in my head seemed

Coming Around from an
Alcohol Induced Psychosis

intensified, as though there was some deep meaning in every little detail.

I left home and managed to make it through to my sister's house in a completely psychotic state of mind. I can vaguely remember that the car seemed to be going all over the road. I imagine my sister was extremely concerned given I spent the night talking to the pictures on the wall shouting, "Alleluia I have been given salvation." I did not know the meaning of salvation, never mind shouting it around her house. I was refusing to eat food because it belonged to the devil. I was telling my sister she needed to get the children out of bed as they were in danger. In short, I was causing complete disruption to her normally sane household.

The next day she 'kindly' took me to Gosforth near Newcastle and dropped me by the roadside. She made a quick departure back home, where she could forget about her horrendous ordeal with me. I know she would never forget this experience as this must have been a complete nightmare for her. Nevertheless, it was clear that she just wanted to get me away from her door, in the hope that someone else would help me out. We later laughed about this. Another important issue here was that she could not

Coming Around from an
Alcohol Induced Psychosis

find it in herself to telephone a doctor; this would have brought back the nightmare memories of our childhood with our mother. I completely understood this.

I can remember doing the strangest things in Gosforth that day. I was walking to places I did not know existed, and looking for a Church. I talked to a number of people on my travels. God only knows what I said to them. At one point the voices told me to jump in front of a bus. The longer I was remaining alcohol free the crazier I was getting. I was perfectly sane when I was drunk. Now sobriety brought me insanity, life did not make a lot of sense. Although to be fair I don't think I had any awareness at that point that what I was doing and saying were insane, although things did not feel normal, I had no insight into the craziness that was going on in my mind. Everything I had to do was right in my head.

It was becoming obvious that my memories of the lead up to "coming around" did not look good. You know when that overwhelming feeling of shame and humiliation pervades your body; well, that is how I felt, as though the ground would swallow me up. Never mind I had to brave more memories to try to get to where I was in terms of coming around.

Coming Around from an Alcohol Induced Psychosis

A horrible thought came flooding back; I remember standing in Jeff's house. Jeff was the man who I had lived with for fourteen years who had repeatedly physically, mentally and emotionally battered and abused me. I will never forget the amount of terror that went through my body that day when he walked into his apartment. I violently shook uncontrollably from head to foot for about half an hour. I was shuddering in every sinew of my being. Again, I think this was some kind of healing experience my body was going through, but it was a scary ordeal. At that point I had a white bible in my hand which I had bought before I reached his place in the hope that it would act as some form of everlasting protection.

Although there is an element of sanity in my recollection of these events, for most part I was hearing voices telling me what to do. In my utterly chaotic, psychotic state of mind I remember him saying he would try to help me; I was sane enough to know that his help would drag me further into the mire, as it always did. I told him how all these years I had only been with him because if I asked him to get out of the house, he would beat me up. He promised that would all change, and he would stop drinking in order to help me. I had listened to his lies, promises and threats

Coming Around from an
Alcohol Induced Psychosis

for fourteen years and was beyond being conned any more. I walked away from him, swearing that he would never come back into my life. I told him I would rather be dead than continue in a relationship with him. For some reason this experience felt final, as though the Bible had acted as some form of deterrent placing a barrier between us which would last forever! Nevertheless, I still felt weird as I recalled the events in his home.

Next, I went to a local metro station in Shiremoor with the white bible which had now turned evil and into a Bible written by the devil. I threw it on the metro line along with my bag, my money and all my belongings. Yes, everything was now turning evil and belonged to the devil. The next day the police had returned them to my son who was still at home wondering where on earth I had disappeared to. I ended up on the Sunday in the Haymarket in Newcastle. Given I now had no bag or money I started the nine mile walk home to my sleepy little village. By the way, the messages I was hearing would not have allowed me to own any money or belongings so in my head there was no hardship about walking nine miles home. It was beginning to get dark; I thought all the cars were spying on me; they were using radio control to keep in touch with each other to

Coming Around from an
Alcohol Induced Psychosis

monitor my moves. I was totally paranoid and psychotic. I walked up to two women talking at the bus stop and told them in no uncertain terms, "I worked for it and paid for it!" Now that is paranoia at its best. God only knows what they thought.

At about eleven o'clock that night I remember starting to collapse. I'd had no food or drink for a couple of days, as in my head this was related to the devil. It's amazing how crazy the mind can get when not connected to reality. My body could not go any further. I had reached the railway crossing at Seghill. I collapsed on the crossing. I can remember a man being there, and helping me through, he looked brilliant. He had the most beautiful face. Where I was lying on the crossing, I could feel a cross on my back. I was choking it was as though I was being strangled. Someone must have telephoned for an ambulance; this man told the ambulance drivers I had to go into the ambulance head-first. He was placing importance on the way things were done. I seemed to be going through some crazy sort of God the devil fight. When people say before you die your whole life goes before you, it certainly did. I can remember my life just going before my eyes. Strangely enough, it was the events that I had a conscience about that were going

Coming Around from an Alcohol Induced Psychosis

through my memory like a video, such as bits of crime I had been involved in. I was making some attempt to apologise to God for my sins and swearing not to do these things again.

After this, I started to catapult back through life, I remember hitting certain ages; 30, 24, 16, 8, 2, and birth. My body then curled up into the foetal position at which point I went into a coma. There did seem to be some strange memories during this coma, both of evil and good. I remember thinking someone was the devil, but I also thought there was an angel there. But alas I have no explanation for what really did happen during that period, as separating reality from delusion or hallucinations during a psychotic episode was never going to happen. This was the three-day coma I was just coming around from on the hospital ward. I also found out later that this was the point that many alcoholics die.

Well reflections over, now I had completed my recap, throwing some light on my situation, and how I had got to where I was, I felt better informed. Believe me being better informed certainly did nothing to make me feel any better. I felt horrified at the thought of some of the crazy things I

Coming Around from an
Alcohol Induced Psychosis

had done during my 'accidental' alcoholic detox leading to
the DTs.

After my recap I was on my feet quickly, and eager to try
to get out of this hospital. I am sure you would have
worked that out for yourself. I still found it quite disturbing
that many of the patients looked pathetic, were lethargic,
and walked with stooped shoulders looking at their feet. I
was terrified in case I was going to end up like them. They
would find out that I had escaped from that psychiatric
hospital in Scotland twelve years earlier and I would now
have to spend the rest of my life locked up in this hospital. I
was sure they got paid extra for keeping patients in long
term.

After I settled down a bit, I tentatively approached a nurse
to explain that I had been dealing with Lydia the social
worker from the Shop Front. I asked if she could 'please'
arrange for her to come to see me to organise my release
from this hospital. At least I now knew that the only way I
would get out of this place would be if I had someone
official on my side that was batting for me. They did get in
touch with her, and she came to see me within a couple of
days. I felt much better after speaking to her, as she said

Coming Around from an Alcohol Induced Psychosis

she would make some enquires as to what help was available for me and would return in a couple of days.

The staff here must have undergone a heart transplant, as they allowed me to go for a walk in the hospital grounds. Believe it or not, I did not try to escape, as I believed that Lydia would come back and help me to move forward. I can remember walking through the grounds and being aware of my experience, it was the first time since I was a young child that I could feel the breeze blowing around my face. I could see the green grass, trees and flowers. I could smell the air and the scents from the flowers dancing on the breeze. The sky was a bright blue with the odd fluffy white cloud moving slowly in the warm autumn breeze. I could feel my feet as they hit the ground when I walked. All my senses were alive for the first time since I was very young. I savoured the experience. Yes, the alcohol was out of my system and I could feel again. This was one of those very special moments in my life; it was the beginning of things to come, which I did not know at that time.

While on the hospital ward there was an elderly woman who had been in the hospital for over forty years. One of the nurses told me she had been admitted as a teenager because she was pregnant and had been kept there ever

Coming Around from an
Alcohol Induced Psychosis

since. She just fitted in with the hospital routine as she was completely institutionalised. At the ward round she just took her medication without question and did not say a word to anyone. Apparently, she had not had a visitor for years; after her admittance her father came in a couple of times and then stopped. I know we hear about cases like this, but it just felt so sad that this woman's only company for the past forty years were the staff on the hospital ward. It was also clear that they really were not interested in forming any kind of real relationship with her.

Well, this woman started to quietly follow me around the hospital. Now don't start to think I was going to stay there to keep her company. No, that was far from my intentions. Nevertheless, I did not think she was taking too much notice of me because she didn't speak. I had tried to speak to her, and all I got was a shy smile. She was never far from my side during the day; she would shuffle along as fast as she could to keep up with me. When I was aware of her shadowing me, I would slow down to allow her to come alongside. She never came alongside, she dropped in behind me, and was obviously happy just staying in the background.

Coming Around from an Alcohol Induced Psychosis

I often quarrelled with the nurses over having to take my medication. Then one day we were all sitting in the ward waiting for the meds trolley to come, and I did my norm, which was to object to having to take any medication. When it came to the old-timer's turn, she said to the nurse, "I am not taking any tablets." The nurses on the meds trolley could not believe their ears - they made such a scene. They shouted on the other nurses on the ward to come in and hear her. Here was a sweet old, institutionalised woman, who always obeyed orders actually arguing with them. I felt so touched by her behaviour, as she was obviously emulating my behaviour. I was never the best example of good behaviour in the world, but I was chuffed to bits.

However, it was not long before my body started to crave the alcohol it was missing. I had been told by the psychiatrist in the hospital that I had damaged my liver. My body was not in good condition as a result of the enormous amounts of alcohol I had drunk over the last seventeen years. The damage to my liver was reversible if I stopped drinking. I was told, "If you continue to drink you will be lucky if you last six months. Make a choice - change or die."

Coming Around from an
Alcohol Induced Psychosis

I could not envisage life without drinking, just in case you didn't guess, it was one of the most important things in my life. Everyone I knew drank; my life had also revolved around bars for the past seventeen years. How on earth was I supposed to give all that up? Nevertheless, there was a part of me that wanted so much to make it without alcohol. I knew how much drink was ruining my life. I felt deep in my heart that I could be successful if I could only escape the lifestyle, I was so immersed in. So once again I have this two-sided fight going on in my head.

I was delighted when Lydia did come back to see me. She said, it would not be wise for me to go home as my drinking and behaviour was so out of control; I would be dead within months if I continued with the life style I was living. She too said, "You need to change or die."

Well, I thought, that was quite some choice they were giving me. At that time in my life I really didn't understand the implications of my life choices. Nevertheless, she was at least going to help me to make the choice, as she suggested I go into a rehabilitation unit which she would arrange. I agreed to this, although I did not have a clue about what this meant. She explained that I would have to go for an interview, and be assessed by the residents and

Coming Around from an
Alcohol Induced Psychosis

staff in the unit. I was told, as soon as she was able to arrange this interview and if I was accepted by the staff and residents I would be discharged from the ward and moved to the rehab. Gosh how times had changed, they were **not** going to try to keep me in this hospital against my will until I died! The most important thing about being released from this hospital meant that they thought I was sane enough to leave! I could now move forward from the previous experience without fearing being locked up again. How happy was I? This was truly the beginning of the rest of my life, I fortunately went on to be very successful but the rest of my story is in my best-selling book, *"Change or Die: Abuse to Addiction to Abundance."* Nevertheless I have not had another drink for over thirty years, nor do I allow abusive people into my life. Well done me!

I would like to say a big thank you for joining me on my journey, and if you have enjoyed my book and hopefully found it useful, can I ask that you please give me a review? This would be greatly appreciated.

All my best wishes Catherine ER Ellison

Printed in Dunstable, United Kingdom